# The Flak Towers Hamburg and Vienna 1940-1950

## Michael Foedrowitz

*Design for Flak Tower (G-Tower) No. IV in 1:50 scale, with a plaque in memory of Oberst Hahns over the entrance.*

**Schiffer Military/Aviation History**
Atglen, PA

## 1. Archives:

ArGe, "Unter den Strassen von Berlin"—Dietmar Arnold; Axel Springer Text Archives (Ullstein, Berlin); Federal Archives—Military Archives, Freiburg; Main State Archives, Düsseldorf; Wedding Homeland Museum, Berlin; State Archives, Berlin; Angerer Collection; Wleklinski Collection; Moscow Special Archives; State Archives, Bremen; State Archives, Hamburg; City Archives, Berlin.

## Photos, Plans, Drawings:

Kronenzeitung Archives, Vienna; Dr. Kriegl Archives; Federal Archives, Koblenz; Michael Foedrowitz Photo Archives; Wedding Homeland Museum, Berlin; State Archives, Berlin; State Photo Agency, Berlin; State Photo Agency, Vienna; State Photo Agency, Hamburg; City Archives, Berlin; Elke Allinger; Henning Angerer; Dietmar Arnold; Dr. Jan Heitmann; Dr. Marcello La Speranza; Michaela Mlcuch; Martin Paterra; Dr. Hans Richter; Gerd Rose; Peter Schmidt; Hans Wolf Tamms; Elmar Widmann; Oliver Wleklinski.

## Information and Interviews:

Mr. Rudolf Hauptner; Dr. Josef Kriegl; Dr. Hans Richter; Mr. Gerhard Rose; Mr. Hans Wolf Tamms; Mr. Elmar Widmann; Mr. Dietmar Arnold.

## Newspapers, Journals and Articles:

Bild, 1/9/1974, "Ein netter Mann sprengt Hamburgs Riesen-Bunker", Der Spiegel, 15/1996, "Beute aus dem Flak-Turm"; Die Presse, 6/26/1993, Wolfgang Freitag, "Brüten, alsschlüpfen und runterfallen"; Die Welt, 5/9/1986, Jörg Stratmann, "Der Koloss, der Kreative anzieht"; Die Welt, 6/26/1993, "Auf den Spuren verschollener Bilder"; Die Woche, 7/5/1944, Wolf Strache, "Drohende Türme"; Die Zeit, 3/6/1992, Günter Wermusch, "Das Geheimnis des kleinen Bunkerberges"; Hamburger Abendblatt, 6/14-15/1990, "Umlegen—auf die sanfte Tour"; Kurier, 3/13/1946, "Berlins Hochbunker—ein Jahr nach dem Kriege"; Tagesspiegel, 2/29/1948, "Humboldtbunker—sehr stabil"; Tagesspiegel, 11/11/1949, "Protest gegen Bunkersprengung"; Telegraf, 12/16/1947, "Humboldtbunker gesprengt"; Wiener Zeitung, 10.28/1989, Franz Severin Berger, "Die grauen Riesen der Macht".

## Books

Banny, Leopold, "Dröhnender Himmel. Brennendes Lend". Vienna, 1988.

Borkowski, Dieter, "Wer weiss, ob wir uns wiedersehen". Frankfurt am Main, 1983.

Girbig, Werner, "Im Anflug auf die Reichshauptstadt". Stuttgart, 1973.

Heitmann, Jan, "Gomorrha—The Hamburg Firestorm", in: After the Battle No. 70. London, 1990.

Hoffmann, Andreas, "Zoobunker", in: Geschichtslandschaft Berlin. Berlin-Tiergarten 1, 1989.

Jirout, H., & J. Späth, "Flakturmprojekt Wien". Berlin 1990 (Dissertation, Technical University of Berlin).

Le Tissier, Tony, "Berlin damals und heute". London, 1994.

———, "Der Kampf um Berlin 1945", Frankfurt/Berlin, 1994.

Müller, Werner, "Deutsche schwere Flak", in: Waffen-Arsenal Special Volume S 15. Friedberg, 1990.

———, "Die Geschütze, Ortungs- und Feuerleitgeräte der schweren Flak", Friedberg, 1988.

Niehaus, Werner, "Die Radarschlacht 1939-1945". Stuttgart, 1977.

Nowarra, Heinz J., "Die deutsche Luftrüstung 1933-1945", Vol. 4. Koblenz, 1933. [date?]

Read, Anthony, & David Fischer, "Der Fall von Berlin". Berlin, 1995.

Riedel, Heide, "Fernsehen—Von der Vision zum Programm". Deutsches Rundfunkmuseum e.V., Berlin, 1985.

Ryan, Cornelius, "Der letzte Kampf". Munich, 1977.

Weber, Klaus Konrad, "Berlin und seine Bauten", Part III, Bauwerke für Regierung und Verwaltung. Militärbauten.

Zhukov, Georgi K., "Erinnerungen und Gedanken". Stuttgart, 1969.

"Zerbrochene Zeit. Wilhelmsburg in den Jahren 1923-1947". Hamburg, Geschichtswerkstatt Wilhelmsburg, 1993.

"Tiergarten Mai 45. Zusammenbruch-Befreiung-Wiederaufbau". Berlin, Tiergarten Homeland Museum, 1995.

"Das Gebäude", Volume 1 of the "Bunker-Berg" Exposition Series, Berlin, Wedding Homeland Museum, 1995-96.

For their technical assistance I extend hearty thanks to Dr. Josef Kriegl, Dr. Marcello La Speranza, Gerhard Rose, Elmar Widmann and Dietmar Arnold of the "ArGe—Unter den Strassen von Berlin". Special thanks to Mr. Elmar Widmann, who undertook, among other things, the laborious proofreading of the manuscript. Special thanks also go to Maria Nizio and Izabela Foedrowitz. I also thank Ms. Elke Allinger, Messrs. Hans Wolf Tamms, Werner Müller, the Wedding Homeland Museum in Berlin, Koziura Hannover Military Library), Peter Schmidt, Henning Angerer, Dr. Jan Heitmann, and all those who helped in this work.

In particular, I thank the GENZ Photo Shop in Hannover.

**Cover photo: The G-Turm, Augarten, taken in May 1996. Copyright Michael Foedrowitz.**
**This work was supported by the GENZ Photo Shop, Hannover.**

Translated from the German by Don Cox

Copyright © 1998 by Schiffer Publishing, Ltd.

Printed in China.
ISBN: 0-7643-0398-8

This book was originally published under the title, *Waffen Arsenal-Waffen und Fahrzeuge der Heere und Luftstreitkräfte* by Podzun-Pallas Verlag.

We are interested in hearing from authors with book ideas on related topics.

Published by Schiffer Publishing Ltd.
4880 Lower Valley Road
Atglen, PA 19310
Phone: (610) 593-1777
FAX: (610) 593-2002
E-mail: Schifferbk@aol.com
Please write for a free catalog.
This book may be purchased from the publisher.
Please include $3.95 postage.
Try your bookstore first.

# Foreword

In the course of World War II, the so-called "Flak towers" were built in Berlin, Hamburg and Vienna. Each consisted of a fire-control and a gun tower. They rank among the largest concrete structures that were built in the German Reich at that time. Reich Propaganda Minister Joseph Goebbels referred to them in his diary as "genuine wonders of defense", and the Americans described the Flak towers as the best of all bunker designs. After the war, wild rumors and speculations grew around the concrete giants: they were linked by secret underground passages (Berlin), or executed Russian prisoners were entombed in their walls (Vienna). All the same, the history of the Flak towers is varying and adventurous, and wavers among air warfare, sacrifice to coldness, robbery of art, and shark pools.

The Flak towers built in Berlin, Hamburg and Vienna during World War II constituted a novelty in military fortification architecture, for never before had similar constructions arisen in Germany.

The nomenclature of the subject is extremely confused and complicated. The concept of the Flak tower always includes a pair of towers: the G or gun tower and the L or fire-control tower. Even renowned historians constantly get them confused and make mistakes. Let it be said in their favor that the pen-pushing bureaucrats of the Third Reich could never agree on a single uniform concept: the G-tower was called the gun or the combat tower, the battery tower or the large Flak tower; the L-tower, on the other hand, was called the command tower, listening bunker, or small Flak tower.

The concept of the Flak tower, according to Elmar Widmann, the best authority on these edifices in the Federal Republic, already existed before World War II; for example, eight Flak towers with a height of thirty meters were planned to protect a new railroad station in Munich. The Japanese also built Flak towers of concrete, some of them to protect airfields on Formosa/Taiwan, but they were not comparable to the German Flak towers in dimensions, design or construction technology.

The Flak towers that are examined here had military and civilian tasks alike: on the one hand, they were supposed to coordinate anti-aircraft defense and also carry out some of it themselves, and on the other hand, they were to provide tens of thousands of civilians with safe air-raid shelters.

In all, there were three "Flak-tower generations"; the first consisted of the three towers in Berlin and Flak Tower IV in Hamburg (Heiligengeistfeld). The second generation consisted of two Flak towers: in Wilhelmsburg (Hamburg) and in the Arenberg Park in Vienna. The third and last generation included the Flak towers at the Stiftskaserne and Augarten (both in Vienna), which differed considerably from the original designs and had already been influenced architecturally by the action and combat experiences of the other Flak towers.

After the first RAF air raid made by 29 bombers on the Reich's capital city on the night of August 25-26, 1940, Hitler himself ordered the construction of Flak towers.

The Führer also saw himself chosen as the architect and artist in the task of designing them, so that he single-handedly prepared drawings of the future Flak towers, which managed to look more like the war memorial built after the war in Tobruk than like the Flak towers in Berlin.

Numerous investigations had to be carried out first. How, for example, would the ground, with its many strata, react to the weight of 100,000 tons? The obligatory test holes drilled before the building of a large bunker would not suffice in this case. Just to answer this question, considerable efforts were made and, for example, gigantic massive concrete structures, "great-pressure bodies", were set up to test the ground (also for the huge triumphal arches that were planned), such as in Charlottenburg.

Originally, six Flak gun towers were planned for Berlin, but only three were actually built. First came the "Zoo" Flak tower, probably the most renowned bunker of any kind in World War II, then came the other two concrete fortresses of Humboldthain and Friedrichshain. All the Berlin Flak towers were alike in their basic details. They were always put up in pairs; with every gun tower (G-tower) there was always a fire-control tower (L-tower). The guns were mounted on the G-tower, the range finders on the L-tower. The latter transmitted their shot values and data to the G-tower through a cable tunnel. In 1941, two pairs of Flak towers were begun in Hamburg as part of the "Special Program Berlin"; the first one built was Flak Tower IV at the Heiligengeistfeld. It was identical to the three Flak towers in Berlin except for a few details. A third pair of towers in eastern Hamburg did not get built. In September 1942, Hitler ordered the erection of Flak towers in Vienna. Plans made in 1942 to erect Flak towers in Bremen as well did not become reality.

The total of eight gun towers, each with its fire-control tower, formed autonomous entities in terms of power and water supply. They included hospitals and art treasures, research laboratories and equipment workshops, radio transmitters and Gestapo stations, air-raid shelters for the civilian population and command posts for the Wehrmacht.

The job of the Flak towers, in addition to coordinating anti-aircraft defense, did not consist primarily of shooting down enemy aircraft, but to hinder their flights over certain areas of the cities, whether the government buildings of Berlin within the triangle of Flak towers built there or the cultural metropolis of Vienna, which Hitler classified as valuable.

The construction design proved itself in the war; almost all the gun towers took direct bomb hits without being damaged. Their military utility, though, did not measure up to what had been hoped for.

After the war, the obviously impressed Allies tried to blow up the Flak towers, but with limited success. The Berlin bunkers were made invisible through small partial explosions, removals and covering with earth ("bunker hills"). Only one part of the Humboldthain gun tower can be seen today, though only from outside. In Hamburg, only the two gun towers are still standing, while in Vienna, on account of the construction situation, all three pairs of Flak towers are still in existence.

Since information on the subject of Flak towers is very hard to come by, and the few available sources often contradict each other, the author asks for criticism, information and additional data from those who know. To study the Viennese Flak towers, Dr. Josef Kriegl requests reliable information and newspaper articles. His address is: Dr. Josef Kriegl, Steinabrunngasse 1/c, A-2405 Bad Deutsch-Altenburg, Austria.

Architect Prof. Friedrich Tamms, designer of the Flak towers, in 1966.

Luftwaffe helpers stand before the twin 128 mm "Dora" Flak gun on the Zoo gun tower in Berlin in 1944.

The position of the former information tower in Tremmen, looking westward. It was torn down in 1945.

Below: A look at the L-tower from the Zoo G-tower in Berlin; at left are the Kaiser Wilhelm Memorial Church and the Händelallee.

# BERLIN

On September 9, 1940, came the command to build the Flak towers in Berlin. In the applicable document from the adjutancy of the Wehrmacht at the Führer's headquarters, six Flak towers were planned: three at the Tiergarten and one each in the Humboldthain, Friedrichshain and in Hasenheide in the Tempelhof district. Each of the towers was to be armed with four 105 mm naval guns in twin mounts, plus several 37 and 20 mm Flak guns. Inside the towers, safe quarters for the gun crews were planned. Albert Speer was to direct the architectural work on the towers. The construction itself was to be carried out by the OT.

But these plans already caused problems. At a meeting in the RLM on September 20, 1940, in which General Steudemann (Inspection of Flak Artillery), General Haubold, Commander of LGK III, Frigate Captain Sorge and twelve other officers plus Dipl.Ing. Körting and Dr. Hentzen of the GBI took part, General Haubold noted in reference to the Flak artillery that 105 mm naval guns were not available, and a 127 mm naval gun would only be available in a year and a half. They would have to get by with available 105 mm Flak guns. In this discussion the technical data were also determined, but they were to be changed much in the actual construction. A Flak tower was supposed to consist of four towers, linked with each other, in the middle of which, with a radial distance of 35 meters, a command device was to be set up. The dimensions were to be 60 x 60 meters, the height 25 meters, "so that the towers rise above the trees of the Tiergarten". At a distance of 400 to 500 meters, or sometimes only 300 meters away from the gun tower, a command tower was to be built, with dimensions of 30 x 30 or 40 x 40 meters. The crew of the L-tower was to consist of 100 men and 6 officers, that of the G-tower 160 men and 6 officers. Bombproof ammunition rooms were to be built with paternoster elevators, plus a kitchen, dining rooms, supply rooms and workrooms, etc. General Rüdel was commissioned to report to Hitler and also to talk about the possibility of erecting battery towers, meaning command towers separated for reasons of technical necessity from the gun towers, and equal to two or three gun towers. After the locations of the Flak towers were discussed in military terms, points relating to the cities were also prought up. Hentzen said: "The Flak towers should, if possible, be brought into connection with building or street axes, in order to give them a monumental connection."

For the architectural designing, the architect Friedrich Tamms, colleague of the GBI and the Inspector-General, was appointed by the Inspector-General for German Roads, Dr. Fritz Todt, on October 1, 1940.

The Inspection of Flak Artillery (Fortification Dept.), on September 23, 1940, announced the results of a discussion by the offices involved in the project. The choice of heavy Flak guns caused several problems, for the Navy could only supply double-barreled 105 mm guns in a year and a half. The naval Flak guns were triaxial, equipped with a loose axis (angled aiming works) to equalize ships' movements, and therefore much more complicated than the usual fixed Flak used on land. For the fixed use of Flak guns, the Navy had developed a 128 mm Flak gun, but this too would only be available in a year and a half. It was suggested that the mounts on the Flak towers be set up for the 128 mm guns and be fitted temporarily with 105 mm types. It was also suggested that 50 mm Flak be used in addition to 20 and 37 mm Flak guns.

In this discussion it also became clear that two towers would have to be built for every tower Flak battery. The main command device and the new radar apparatus had to be kept at a distance of 300 to 500 meters from the heavy guns. The Navy had also confirmed this. So there had to be a "battery tower" (gun tower, G-tower) with the four heavy guns and a secondary command post (B) plus light Flak, as well as a command tower with a primary command post, equipped with the main command device, electric measuring device, hearing device, perhaps searchlights, etc. On the L-tower there should also be light Flak guns, and the use of the Command Device 40 on the G-tower should be limited to times when the Command Post B I was not working.

The dimensions of the Flak towers were determined by the heavy Flak guns. They had to be set at least 35 meters from B (command post) II, and the distance between guns had to be 50 to 70 meters. Every heavy Flak gun would need a platform of 10 x 10 meters. The light Flak weapons were to be mounted lower, so as not to affect the operation of the heavy units, and so their crews would not be exposed to the muzzle noise of the planned 128 mm guns. Another possibility was that of placing the light Flak and the command device on a raised platform in the center of the Flak tower, but this would mean that in combat action with low gun elevation, one gun would be out of action. In order to guarantee the stability of the towers, they had to be widened by 20 x 20 meters downward. A gun weight of some 30 tons and a recoil power of 25 tons were expected. Under the platforms, readiness rooms, living quarters and workrooms were to be built, plus room for ammunition and equipment and the necessary elevators and machine rooms.

The "command tower" (fire-control or L-tower) should have a platform of 10- to 15-meter diameter. Light Flak guns and searchlights should be mounted somewhat lower. In the L-tower would be living quarters, readiness and storage rooms, the battery command post, and rooms for the dissemination of intelligence reports.

Both towers should not be built near other buildings, "in order to avoid shot damage to the gun towers and echo interference at the command tower.

In terms of city planning, there plans were more complicated. If the Führer's command were to be followed and three Flak towers built in the Tiergarten, then the three L-towers would have to be added. The Inspection of Flak Artillery noted on September 23, 1940: "It will be a difficult task for the General Building Inspector to bring these six towers into a harmonious accord with the other existing and planned buildings and monuments in the Tiergarten." The integration of these structures into the Tiergarten would be simpler if they could be limited to only two pairs.

As for the Tiergarten, the site was limited to one G- and one L-tower. Architect Tamms, though, was concerned about the animals in the zoological gardens, whom [p. 6] the loud noise would cause to "suffer so much that they would presumably perish in time." But since the zoo was to be moved anyway, the problem of the animals was regarded as solved. A suggestion by Tamms to move the planned location of the Flak tower was turned down.

The north side of the Zoo G-tower, near the Zoo depot in the Tiergarten district of Berlin.

On October 25, 1940, Tamms presented a ground plan in 1:2000 scale, nine drawings and a 1:200 scale model in a discussion with Speer. Speer agreed essentially with his designs. On March 6, 1941, Speer turned over detailed drawings and two 1:50 scale models to Speer. Speer agreed to the architectural designs. But there were difficulties with the stone facings over the granite foundation. These were to be made of French limestone or German sandstone. Later Speer passed a request of Hitler on to Tamms, calling for the attachment of large tablets bearing the names of German aviation heroes at all the entrances of the ZOO Flak tower.

As structures important to the war, the Flak towers were rated in the highest category of urgency. The Flak Tower I with sections A (gun tower) and B (command tower) were located by the Zoo and bore the official number OX Berlin I. On March 6, 1941, the building costs were calculated at 5.5 million Reichsmark, which seems to be a reduced amount for the "Zoo Bunker" which was already under construction. Flak Tower II in Friedrichshain, with sections D (gun tower) and E (command tower), was calculated at 24 million Reichsmark. It bore the official number OX Berlin 3. Including the other structures that went with it (service facilities, access and other structures), it was given the O level of urgency rating.

In Tremmen in Havelland, some 40 kilometers west of Berlin, an intelligence tower (Structure C) was built; it cost 500,000 Reichsmark and had the number OX Berlin 2. The first German panoramic scope was installed there and linked by direct cable to the command post of the 1st Flak Division, to supply targeting information (range 300 km) on approaching enemy aircraft at all times.

In 1941 a plan was made to rebuild the Reichstag Building as a Flak tower. This building, made of Silesian granite, likewise had four corner turrets that seemed to be suitable for the installation of Flak positions. The rebuilding was to begin on July 1, 1941; the tower on the cupola and the sculptures were to be removed!

# Flak Tower Zoo
## G-Tower

The construction of the most famous Flak tower, the so-called "Zoo Bunker", began. The Inspector of the Flak Weapons, Generalleutnant Steudemann, had given the order for it on September 9, 1940. The Reichsbahn guaranteed two trains a day to bring 1600 tons of building materials, while 500 tons a day were delivered by waterways.

After the concrete work of the G-tower was finished, the German Reichsbahn, using heavy tractors and low loaders, delivered the 71-ton armored ammunition elevators. The Flak tower had a permanent crane installed on the lower platform over its main entrance, but it could not lift this weight, since it was only built to lift ten tons.

Thus, a crane apparatus was built, and the armored cupolas were lifted to the gun platforms and placed over the ammunition elevator shafts.

The ground surface of the G-tower measured 70.5 x 70.5 meters. The cubic outer walls were 2.5 meters thick, tapering to two meters upward. Later the Flak tower was given a gray-green coat of paint. The tower had one cellar, one ground floor and five upper floors. The floors were linked by spiral staircases in the corners of the tower. There was also a staircase in the center of the Flak bunker, as well as several other flights of stairs. There were two freight elevators, which could only be used for military purposes or for moving injured personnel to the hospital. Sometimes the elevators were also used as "holding cells" for Luftwaffe helpers.

The Flak bunker was designed to shelter 8000 civilians, but it was reported that during air raids, 30,000 people found shelter there (planned places: 15,000). For the civilian population, three entrance doors, 4 by 6 meters, were available, but these proved to be too small for the crowds of people. Later a wooden staircase was erected on brick pillars over the western entrance, by which direct access to the first upper floor could be attained. Among the Berliners, the "Zoo-Bunker" was known as "the safest coffin in the world".

In the second upper story, art treasures from fourteen Berlin museums were stored in fully air-conditioned rooms. They included the golden treasures of Priam, the coin collection of Kaiser Wilhelm and the bust of Nefretiti. Albert Speer had made these rooms available to Otto Kümmel, Director of the Prussian Museums, on June 10, 1941. In August 1941, the pergament frieze was placed in the Flak tower. For a year, trucks brought the most valuable art treasures to the concrete castle, where they were stored in 1500 square meters. Since the security of the storage place decreased toward the end of the war, the Museum directors decided to have the cultural materials evacuated to mine shafts, and began to remove them on March 22, 1945.

In the third upper story, a hospital with 95 beds and two operating rooms was set up. Eight doctors, twenty nurses and thirty aides did their work here. Prominent persons of the times were treated there: Hanna Reitsch, who was wounded in an air raid at the end of 1943, Generaloberst Schmundt, who was seriously injured in the attempted assassination of July 20, 1944, and the fighter pilot Hans-Ulrich Rudel, who was shot down on the Oder in February 1945 and visited in the hospital by Goebbels and Göring.

The entire Flak personnel had their quarters in the fourth upper floor.

In April 1941 the two Zoo Flak towers were ready for action. General Kressmann, as commander of the 1st Flak Division, had set up his command post in the L-tower, as did General Sydow in December 1944, after Kressmann's death. Although the specifications were secret, not everything could be concealed. For example, when the "Würzburg Giant" was installed on the L-tower, [p. 10] photos were taken secretly by members of the American embassy.

Berliner humor

The command post on the Zoo G-tower. On the L-tower is the "Würzburg Giant", and the Victory Column is seen at right.

Model of the Zoo gun tower.

The heavy armored cupolas for the ammunition elevators were brought to the G-tower by heavy Reichsbahn transporters. A crane mounted on the outside wall lifted the 72-ton cupolas to the highest platform.
Widmann: "Next to every 128 mm position was one of those 72-ton steel boxes in which the ammunition elevators ended. They could be closed by heavy steel doors. Originally, every 128 mm position was also supposed to have a smaller, similar steel box on the opposite side; but the stairways that ended in them served only to remove empty shell casings." Only in G-towers I and II were two smaller elevators installed.

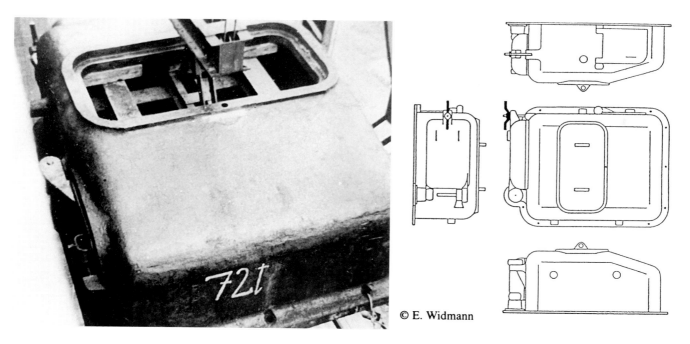

© E. Widmann

The 72-ton steel cupolas were positioned to give access to the 128 mm positions. The smaller elevators in the Humboldthain (Berlin) and Heiligengeistfeld (Hamburg) G-towers were omitted altogether. Lower left: One of the steel cupolas for the large ammunition elevators, shown in the blowing up of the Zoo G-tower.

© LAB

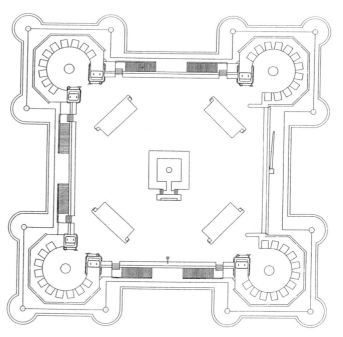

Ground plan of the uppermost platform of the Friedrichshain gun tower. Below: cupolas for small elevators.

The G-tower had its own deep-level reservoir and was independent of the city water supply system. The Flak tower was also autonomous in terms of electrical supply. A large kitchen and a bakery were also included. Military experts later stated that the Zoo Flak fortress could have held out for a year after the German surrender, regardless of what else had happened in Berlin. This view, though, is not tenable.

At first, 88 mm Flak guns were to be positioned on the G-tower (according to Peter Schmidt, Werner Girbig, "Im Anflug auf die Reichshauptstadt", p. 154, though in the view of Flak specialist Gerhard Rose this is not correct), with 20 mm quads and 37 mm Flak guns on the terraces. In time, 128 mm Flak 44 were also installed on the G-tower. As of August-September 1942, the 128 mm Flak guns in twin mounts, which were built by Hanomag, and which Hitler said were the "most beautiful weapons ever built", arrived. The Flak quads were replaced by triple Flak guns, which were really intended for outpost patrol boats of the Navy. The battery chief of the 1st Battery, Flak Unit 123 (T), on the gun tower was Oberleutnant Maschewski.

The 128 mm Flak 40 was one of the most effective anti-aircraft guns in World War II, but in 1944-45, at the beginning of the rocket age, which had also begun in anti-aircraft weapons by then, it was no longer sufficient. The shot height was 14,800 meters, the maximum range 20,950 meters. The rate of fire was 20-24 rounds per minute for the twin version (10-12 rounds per barrel). The range of traverse was 360 degrees, that of elevation was from -3 to +88 degrees. The weight ready to fire was 27 tons. By 1945, 34 of the twin versions had been built and used almost exclusively as a tower gun; only in the "Bunä" area were 128 mm Flak guns in twin mounts to be used on the ground in 1944-45, but this never happened. The 128 mm twin had its traversing mechanism on the right side and its elevation apparatus on the left (stepless Pittler-Thoma drive with electric motor). It was loaded electrically. The tower guns were said to be controlled by seismographs.

The Flak guns were controlled by the Command Device 40. In good visibility, optical sightings were used; in bad weather conditions, firing was done by radar values. Shot data from the Friedrichshain and Humboldthain L-towers could also be called in if needed (through the "Malsi" reevaluating device).

Sometimes the tower guns even took part in air combat. In one case, a Messerschmitt 109 was shot down by mistake, but its pilot was able to land unharmed on the East-West Axis.

Salvo fire was done by a definite process, so that sixteen shells exploded in a space of 240 meters, the so-called "windows". Among other things, the heavy tower Flak in Berlin assured that the Allies had to attack the Reich capital in much greater numbers than before.

At first the Flak guns were operated by Luftwaffe soldiers of the Flak artillery; as of 1943, Luftwaffe helpers were used, as well as Ukrainian volunteers and a unit of Russian war prisoners. The crews of the two towers numbered some 500 men, 200 of them in the L-tower.

In 1943 the G-tower took at least one heavy bomb hit, which killed and wounded members of the gun crews. Losses were also caused by firebombs.

In the final combat around Berlin in 1945, the command post of the 16th PGD (Oberst von und zu Gilsa) moved into the L-tower.

As of 4/21/1945, the whole area around the Zoo bunker was under heavy Soviet howitzer fire. The heavy Soviet battery stationed in Marzahn was fired on, at a distance of 12 kilometers, by the 128 mm Flak guns on the tower. At the Flak tower, 500 Soviet shots were counted, while the tower guns themselves fired 400 rounds toward Marzahn. In the course of the further combat, the tower guns are also said to have shot down Soviet tanks.

On April 25, 1945, 64 members of the 18th Medical Company, under Senior Staff Doctor Werner Starfinger, reached the gun tower. To relieve the Luftwaffe hospital, the division doctor set up a second hospital. The dead were buried by the doctors and medics in single and mass graves around the bunker.

At this time, the Zoo Flak tower was constantly being attacked and fired on by Soviet aircraft. Marshal Zhukov said of the bulwark of opposition in Berlin: "The advance of our troops into the heart of Berlin was hindered by a series of other conditions. . . . We also encountered the five-story bunkers, that were 36 meters high with walls one to three meters thick. For the field artillery, these bunkers were invulnerable. On their roofs, Flak artillery was usually set up, which attacked not only our aircraft but also tanks and accompanying infantry. . . . These bunkers . . . formed the main support for the defense of the center of Berlin." In this combat, the tower of the Kaiser Wilhelm Memorial Church was hit by Flak fire by accident.

At the end of March 1945, the main switchboard for the telephone reports of the tank warning service moved in.

In April 1945, the only radio link from the surrounded city came through the Zoo gun tower. Via this link, Hitler sent out the question: "Where is Wenck?" On April 25, 1945, the Defense Commander or Berlin, General Weidling, visited Sydow, the commander of the 1st Flak Division, who was attacked by Soviet bombers shortly thereafter. The tall tower shuddered under the explosions of the bombs that detonated in the area. In the Zoo bunker there were more than 2000 soldiers and countless civilians. The Luftwaffe doctor, Dr. Walter Hagedorn, estimates their numbers at 30,000. Dead bodies and amputated limbs could no longer be removed from the bunker, which was constantly under fire. In the gun tower there were more than 500 dead and 1500 wounded. Shortly before the crew of the Zoo bunker surrendered, a wave of suicides ran through the concrete colossus. The gun tower was turned over to the Soviets by Oberst Wöhlermann, at 12:30 AM on May 2, the command tower at 5:00 AM.

### The Command Tower

Both the Zoo G-tower and the L-tower had been finished in April 1941. On the control platform, one FuSE 65 "Würzburg Giant" and one FuMG 39T had been installed. The "Würzburg Giant" had a range of some 80 kilometers and a range-finding precision [p. 12] of 15-20 meters. The radar equipment was protected by light Flak guns of Tower Flak Unit 123 (Oberstleutnant Karl Hoffmann) on the lower platform.

Taking the cure by looking into the cannon's mouth on the highest platform of the Zoo gun tower.

The crane from the Flohr firm, which could lift tons of weight, served only to hold a washline.

The command post of the 1st Flak Division was housed in the L-tower. From there came the announcements on the radio lines: "Attention, attention, this is the command post of the 1st Flak Division . . . enemy bomber packs are approaching via the Hannover-Braunschweig area. . . . We'll be back." Since the autumn of 1944, the Luftwaffe Intelligence Unit 121, under Oberstleutnant Frikke, was also present.

On the L-tower there was an observation post for some twelve persons. Party officials or high-ranking representatives of the government like Albert Speer watched the spectacle of the aerial combat over Berlin from there. Speer said: "The attacks on Berlin offered an unforgettable scene from the Flak tower."

In April 1945, the artillery commander for the defense of Berlin, Oberstleutnant Platho, moved into the L-tower, and was relieved by Oberst Wöhlermann on April 25.

### After 1945
Dr. Hagedorn remained in the Zoo gun tower until September 1945; then the departments of the Robert Koch Hospital of Moabit moved into the Flak tower, with the typhus department on the first upper floor, surgery on the second, and dysentery on the third. On the fourth floor, Prof. Dr. Siebert attacked typhus and dysentery. The "Zoo Bunker" took in 330 patients, but a capacity of 500 was planned. At this point in time (March 1946), the Flak guns were still present. In the winter, the tower also served as a refuge for the homeless. Then the British ordered the gun tower evacuated as of April 15, 1947. On June 28, 1947 the L-tower was blown up, and the G-tower was likewise to be demolished. The first two attempts (8/30/1947 and 9/27/1947) were failures. Then 435 holes were drilled in the concrete walls with oxygen torches. After four months of preparation, the explosion, using 35 tons of dynamite, was carried out at 12:24 on July 30, 1948. this time it was successful. The Zoo buildings were damaged as a result; the animals were evacuated twice, to be sure, but many animal houses and enclosures were badly damaged. Explosives master Hans Jürgen Marquardt was in charge of the demolition of the G-tower, and was later to demolish the Heiligengeistfeld L-tower in Hamburg. In 1950-51, the resulting mountain of rubble was planted over, though without much success. On April 18, 1955, the Senate decided to have the rubble trucked away for the construction of the planned Line G (now 9) of the subway. The material (412,000 cubic meters of rubble) was ground up and used for road construction. The gain equalized the costs, in the amount of four million Marks. Only in 1969 were the remains of the foundation removed. Today the grounds of the former L-tower are home to the bird-preserve island of the Zoo, while the area of the G-tower is occupied by the hippopotamus enclosure of the Zoological Gardens.

*The boreholes for the explosive are drilled.*

*Clouds of smoke rise out of the the Zoo G-tower.*

*A clap of thunder and clouds of dust on July 30, 1948.*

*In the foreground is the already demolished L-tower.*

*This once-impressive concrete giant lies in ruins. A few years later, nothing more of the gun tower would be seen.*

*The demolished L-tower; at left is the viewing position, next to it the range-finding platform, the mount for the "Würzburg" device, and at right the shaft for the "Würzburg Giant". The L-tower also disappeared completely.*

*Preparations are made on 11/22/1952 for the demolition of the Zoo L-tower. Boreholes are being bored in the protective shield for the range finder.*

*On the same day. a small explosion took place on the upper platform of the Zoo L-tower.*

# The Friedrichshain Flak Tower

A discussion took place on January 20, 1941, to determine the location of Flak Tower II Friedrichshain. The armament construction department of the Reich Minister for Armament and Ammunition presented plans. The L-tower was planned for the middle of the park, some 350 meters away from the G-tower. The G-tower was to stand right behind the fairytale fountain in the sharp angle of the park between the Friedensstrasse and the Strasse am Friedrichshain. But because of a large HJ home that was planned, the locations were changed. The gun tower was to stand some 400 meters from the west side of the Horst Wessel Hospital, the L-tower directly north of the hospital, between it and the corner of Werneuchenerstrasse, about 350 meters away from the G-tower.

As of April 1941, a G-tower standing 39 meters high, with an equally tall L-tower, arose in the Friedrichshain. In this Flak tower as well, art treasures from Berlin museums would later be stored. On February 3 and 26, 1945, the Flak tower was hit by bombs; when it was built on February 3, only three members of the "Caesar" gun crew survived. The civilians who sought shelter in the tower noticed the bombing only to the extent that some soldiers appeared on the stairs and people became uneasy.

## The L-Tower

In the Friedrichshain L-tower, the commander of Tower Flak Unit 123, the last being Oberstleutnant Karl Hoffmann, had his command post.

Since the autumn of 1944, works of art were also brought into the L-tower. The 1,636 costliest paintings from the Kaiser Wilhelm Museum were kept there.

In the morning hours of May 2, 1945, there was an attempt to break out. Oberstleutnant Hoffmann and his tower crew took part in breaking through the ring of Soviet troops. On the same day, the L-tower was occupied by Soviet troops. The museum guards had left the command post when a bomb had hit the cable tunnel and put out the lights. But when the director of the Liau Museum personnel visited on May 6, he found that the first floor of the L-tower was burned out. On May 18, the scrap depot on the second and third floors was also found to be burned out. Apparently 411 old masters had been lost, but later some pictures from this group turned up at art auctions.

## After 1945

Without any further resistance, the remaining doctor of the hospital surrendered both towers to the Red Army on the morning of May 2, 1945.

The Soviets first blew up the gun tower on April 29, 1946, and on May 2, 1946, they used enough explosive to make the gun tower break in the middle. From 1947 to 1950, rubble and ruins were piled up at the gun tower by "necessity workers", using a rail line. Today the "Big Bunker Hill" is 79 meters high, and only the top of Position A and a part of the western wall can be seen.

*For the pictures on the following pages:*
*From model (above) to ruin (below) in 1949; the Friedrichshain gun tower. Center: photograph, probably from the summer of 1942, showing the gun tower equipped with single 105 mm Flak guns; originally double-barreled 105 Flak guns were planned. In the left part of the lower platform, wooden frames can be seen. No steel blinds have yet been attached to the window openings, but the white cutouts for the frames of the armored doors, 6 cm thick, 2.1 meters high and 1.07 meters wide, can be seen. The insides of the window openings were protected by steel screens.*

*Photo of a 1:20 scale model made in 1943. The rounded outer "swallows' nests" on the corners of the lower platform can be seen clearly. The B II command post had a square concrete wall for protection, like the Humboldthain G-tower, unlike the Zoo G-tower, where the B II was protected by a circular concrete wall.*

*The Friedrichshain control tower, with rounded "swallows' nests", similar to those on the G-tower, on the corners of its lower platform. On the upper platform are the concrete fixtures and protective walls for the radar equipment. Note that in this model the L-tower has two cranes, one on each platform. The upper one is mobile on rollers, the lower, on the other hand, is fixed in place.*

# The Humboldthain Flak Tower

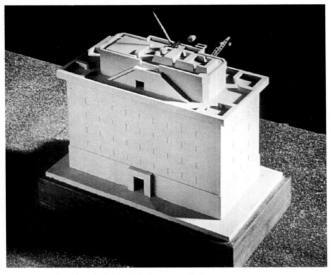

*Model of the Humboldthain L-tower with two cranes.*

### Humboldthain Flak Tower
On June 19, 1941, Architect Tamms visited the site of the Humboldthain Flak tower with Fritz Todt and others. The L-tower was to be built on Gustav-Meyer-Allee in a small rose garden, so that, as Hentzen wrote in a letter to Speer, it would "not look so bad".

### The G-Tower
The G-tower stood northwest of the L-tower. Only two or three trees had to be cut down and the two towers would have a good view of each other.

The price of land in Humboldtshain was given as 14 RM per square meter. The property was taken over by the Wehrmacht in December 1943, when the flak tower was already built. The property amounted to 16,400 square meters and was to be retained until three months after the war ended.

The Humboldthain Flak tower was built between October 1941 and April 1942 and cost some 90 (?) million Marks. As for the actual construction time, the sources disagree; some speak of a time of eleven months, others of seven. The foundation of the

*The Humboldthain L-tower; on the top tower are the "Würzburg Giant" at left, the "Mannheim" radar apparatus in the center and the ten-meter R 43 range finder at right. The white lines were painted for the aiming gunners of the light Flak guns on the lower platform.*

five-story building was two meters thick, or 2.5 meters according to other sources. The outer walls are said to have been two meters thick, or in some places only one. The concrete was reinforced with spiral metalwork. The construction was done by the OT, under the direction of a Herr Zielke. At least 800 workers were brought in for the job: French war prisoners, Hollanders, Italians, Belgians and Yugoslavs. They were housed in barracks between the G- and L-towers. After the G-tower had been finished, 105 mm Flak guns were raised to the upper platform and installed. The police and Luftwaffe had already closed off a large area, though some sources say they used only a normal construction fence. In the

night of January 16-17, 1943, the tower guns saw their first action.

The first armament of the tower, from January to August 1943, consisted of four heavy 105 mm Flak guns, which were later replaced by 128 mm Flak in twin mounts. At the corners of the gallery stood 37 mm Flak guns, with additional 20 mm Flak quads on the sides. These were replaced in 1944 by 37 mm Flak 43 guns, which often malfunctioned, causing much barrel damage. In 1945 these 37 mm Flak 43 guns were removed and replaced by anti-aircraft machine guns. The tower guns on the Humboldthain bunker are said to have shot down 32 planes by the end of the war.

The Humboldthain gun tower, recognizable by the angled-off corners of the lower platform.

This model shows the south side of the Humboldthain G-tower with its crane. Only on this side were there no steps from the lower to the upper platform.

In an average air raid, 400 rounds were fired by the 128 mm Flak guns on the tower. At first camouflage nets were placed over the gun positions, but because of the frequent air-raid alarms they were soon removed. The gun tower itself never was given camouflage paint except on the corner turrets.

Until 1944, searchlight batteries were posted on wooden towers around the Humboldthain G-tower. At first there were four light searchlights of 60 cm diameter (AEG, Wiesenstrasse, Groterjahn, Danzigerstrasse). But they were not sufficient, since their range was only some 2,400 meters, while the air raids were often flown at 11,000 meter heights. They were removed in 1944.

There were three entrances (north, south and east) to the ground floor, one of which could even take trucks and ambulances. On the second floor were the hospital as well as the Women's Service maternity ward, where numerous babies were born during air raids.

Museum objects were stored on the third floor. There were two freight elevators in the G-tower, with a carrying capacity of 24 persons each. To supply the L- and the G-tower with energy, there were a Diesel engine and two emergency generators. As for the ventilation, Herr Rose, who was the training leader for 128 mm Flak guns in Berlin then, reports an interesting detail: "The bunkers ventilated themselves, and the air louvers and the air ducts that went with them were built so cleverly that the warmest rays of the sun warmed the air on one side and this reacted with the cool air on the other side to create a constant circulation of warmed air in the bunker."

In the G-tower (Tower A) there was also a "gas room" set up, in which gas masks were tested.

The gun crews were recruited from Letzte Hoffnung (Last Hope) Luftwaffe helpers, the first eighteen arriving from the Kirschner School in Moabit on February 15, 1943. On June 7, 1944 there were also Luftwaffe helpers from the Vogtland in the tower; they suffered losses in two low-flying air raids.

The Flak guns belonged to Tower Flak Unit 123, which had its command post in the Friedrichshain L-tower. The chief of the heavy battery was named Meyer. The first battery (Schubert, later Düppert) was manned by 31 students from the NWS French Academy. The fifth battery (which was later combined with the sixth as the third battery) consisted of 49 Luftwaffe helpers born in 1926-27 from the Friedrichswerder School. Their schooling continued in the Flak tower until April 15, 1945.

Also among the Flak crews were thirty Ukrainians, who wore blue and yellow armbands. Russian prisoners of war also worked in the G-tower, wearing the letters SU on their uniforms. They worked in the workshops, the writing room, and in the clothing and laundry rooms.

In June 1944, the light tower guns saw dramatic service, firing on two American long-distance fighters that were pursuing an Fw-190. Both planes were shot down, though a nearby chimney was also destroyed by the Luftwaffe helpers.

The G-tower is said to have been hit three times by bombs, but they caused no further damage; not even cracks were observed. On March 18, 1945, the G-turn was hit hard by two bombs, and two guns were knocked out. The G-tower was hit more often by firebombs, but they were simply shoveled over the edge.

The L-tower was hit once by a bomb.

For the people of Berlin, the Flak towers were places of safe shelter from Allied bombs. In the Humboldthain Flak tower it is said that forty thousand people sought shelter, being able to enter it through an underground passage linking it to the Gesundbrunnen railroad station. There are, though, statements that question the existence of this passage.

At that time the bunker was regarded as "indestructible". In the last combat around Berlin, numerous soldiers made their way to the Flak bunker. There the commander of the local defense sector "G", Oberst Schäfer, had his command post. The combat troops of the 12th Soviet Guard Corps, pursuing the Germans, fell before the Flak tower. The tower guns took the enemy units under fire, and shock troops made attacks outward from the Humboldthain. The Soviet artillery systematically fired on the Flak tower, and many Luftwaffe helpers were killed or wounded. The steel blinds, six centimeters thick, were fired on particularly. After a time, some armored doors were shot away and the shells went inside the Flak tower. From nearby buildings, Russian sharpshooters took up the fight against the gun crews on the tower. T-34 tanks in formation fired steadily. Civilians moved two long-barreled Russian guns into position to fire on the concrete. They had no success. On April 23, 1945, the crews were ready to blow up the Flak guns, but the surrender negotiations were concluded only on May 3, 1945. At 12:00 the crew surrendered the Humboldthain Flak tower.

## L-Tower

The L-tower, like the other first-generation command towers, covered an area of 50 x 23 meters. Civilians seeking shelter from air raids also found it in the L-tower.

The transmission of data from the "Würzburg Giant" radar to the G-tower was carried out directly by telephone. The shot values were carried by cable to the Shot Indicator System 37. The information cables ran through a cable tunnel, measuring 1.5 by 1.5 meters, through which power supply cables also ran.

In the L-tower there were also technicians of the Telefunken and Görtz firms, who were there to improve the efficiency of the command post. On the upper platform, the following devices were installed: the eight-ton "Würzburg Giant" with a radar dish 7.5 meters in diameter, the FuMG 64 (Ansbach Device) which removed disturbances from the "Würzburg Giant", the "Würzlaus" (installed as of August 1943 to counteract the strips of foil called "windows" dropped by the British), and the Command Device 40, which was operated by fourteen Flak helpers. The "Würzburg Giant" could be lowered on an elevator into a shaft some 12 meters deep shortly before an air raid began, so it would not be damaged. The technical radar data were then provided by the "Würzburg Device". In addition, another radar device of the "Mannheim" type is said to have been installed on the L-tower. There was also a Command Device 40, with a range-finder with a ten-meter base. In good weather conditions, one could see up to 35 kilometers. Mr. N. served there in "reevaluation". "That was a corner room with two window openings. There we did our work when we had sighted and engaged a definite target. On a piece of paper on a round table, we entered the technical data of the path of the plane to be attacked."

The south side of the Humboldthain G-tower. The trees in front of the Flak bunker were still supposed to be cut down. The 128 mm Flak guns in twin mounts are already in place.

The entrance to the south side of the Humboldthain G-tower. Ambulances could unload patients in the bunkers directly in front of the elevators. Trucks brought Flak ammunition into the bunker, to be taken to the gun platforms by meandering ammunition elevators. Next to the entrance at right are transport cases of 128 mm Flak ammunition. The power lines seem to be temporary, as a makeshift utility pole stands at left near the entrance. The square ventilation hatches to the left and right of the entrance are closed, but some of the steel blinds in front of the windows are open. On hearing an air-raid alarm, the civilian population streamed into the Humboldthain Flak bunker to find protection, especially many mothers with baby carriages. According to reports, toward the end of the war up to 40,000 civilians sought shelter in the Humboldthain G-tower.

The Humboldthain gun tower, seen after its destruction on March 13, 1948. While the south side is completely broken down, only a part of the north wall has been pushed outward by the explosive power of 25 tons of explosive. The upper part remains to this day. The south side is fully caved in (below). The command post B II can be seen clearly on the upper platform.

Range-finding and reporting specialists also analyzed Allied navigational equipment on the first upper floor of the L-tower. Apparatus was brought to the L-tower from shot-down enemy aircraft, including parts of the legendary "Rotterdam Device", which had been assembled and developed further by employees of the Telefunken firm. This device was also used on the L-tower under combat conditions.

## After 1945

After the surrender on May 3, 1945, when all the men in the Flak tower between the ages of 16 and 60 had been taken prisoner, Soviet troops were quartered in the Flak tower. On October 25, 1947, the first explosion in the Humboldthain Flak tower was carried out by the French troops quartered there. On December 13, 1947, they blew up the L-tower with sixteen tons of dynamite. On February 28, 1948, another attempt was made to blow up the G-tower, and part of the outer wall was destroyed, but the Flak tower still stood. On March 13, 1948, a third explosion was carried out, this time with 25 tons of explosives.

The northern part of the Flak tower, with both corner towers, remained intact while the southern part was destroyed. Now the ruin was covered with rubble, and in 1950 1,300 workers were put to work on the "Rubble Mountain Building Site"; among other things, they planted vegetation on it. In the same year, the "German Alpine Society" used the north side of the Flak tower as a "practice Matterhorn". In 1956 it was suggested that the gallery projecting over the mountain of rubble be torn down and the hollow towers be filled with the rubble. In 1986, plans were still being made to tear down the ruin, but it was decided that the remaining part of the Flak tower, which still projects over the mountain of rubble, which is now covered with vegetation, be made into a memorial and viewing platform at a cost of three million Marks. The work was finished on October 28, 1990.

*The Humboldthain G-tower, photographed in 1995. On the northeast tower is the 1.5-ton sculpture "Reunification", made by sculptor Arno Schatz and dedicated on August 12, 1967.*

# Heiligengeistfeld Flak Tower

*A model of the Heiligengeistfeld gun tower in Hamburg.*

## Hamburg

In Hamburg, two pairs of Flak towers, out of the three units originally planned, were built: on the Heiligengeistfeld and in Wilhelmsburg. The gun towers were not identical in design. One Flak-tower pair in eastern Hamburg, which would have formed as "Flak-tower triangle" as in Berlin or Vienna, was never built. The construction was carried out by the military construction department of the Reich Ministry for Armament and Ammunition. According to plans of April 18, 1942, the architects were Vogdt and Hilliger.

Dr.Ing. Friedrich Tamms informed the GBI on February 7, 1942, that Hitler had ordered the building of a fourth Flak tower in Hamburg and the work would begin soon; the preparations had been begun. Flak Tower IV was to be built according to the plans worked out by Tamms for Berlin Flak towers.

According to the building plans, the following arrangements were foreseen in the various floors of the building: On the ground floor of Tower 4 the heating system, in Tower I the air conditioning (fresh air) system, in Tower 2 the water works and in Tower 3 the air exhaust system were planned. In the first upper floor Tower 1 was to have a gas-protection system, the first and second upper floors of Towers 2 and 3 were planned as storage for art treasures. In the second upper story of Tower 4 was the sick bay, in the third upper floor the kitchen and dining facilities were planned, as well as space for the Fluko and Wako. In the fourth upper story were the quarters for the gun crews.

### Hamburg-Heiligengeistfeld

### The Command Tower

The gun and command towers were built between late April and October 1942. According to other sources, the command tower is said to have been built by some 1,000 workers in 350 days. The five-story L-tower measured 50 x 23 meters and was as high as its "big brother". On its uppermost platform was the "Würzburg Giant" radar apparatus.

Its building required 30,000 cubic meters (76,000 tons) of concrete. Confiscated Danish gravel was used. Shortly before the war ended, the Gestapo moved into the command tower (Feldstrasse) bringing prisoners with them.

In 1949 the NWDR occupied two floors of the command tower. The technical director, Werner Nestler, was able to employ numerous specialists and get the work underway.

The studio was a 20-square-meter room in the higher story. On July 12, 1950, the first TV test pattern could be transmitted from the flak tower.

In 1973 the L-tower was sold by the government to the postal system, which had the bunker torn down and a new building erected. In 1973-75 the L-tower (Hochhaus II) on the Budapester Strasse was demolished by Demolition Master Hans Jürgen Marquardt, who used very small charges (260 charges of 20 kg each). Marquardt had already gained experience in Berlin, where he had demolished the "Zoo Bunker" Flak tower. The work in Hamburg was difficult, for the concrete had attained its greatest firmness after thirty years. Thus, massive explosions were not possible, and they would have destroyed the main sewers under the Flak tower. A 22-ton excavator was placed on the roof. At first a 3 x 3 meter shaft was excavated. In all, the demolition required 330 days. Today a Telekom telephone building stands on the site of the L-tower.

### The Gun Tower

The G-tower (officially called "Flak Tower IV Hamburg") had a surface area of 70.5 x 70.5 meters and was some 39 meters high. It stood on a foundation plate 2.5 meters thick. The walls were 2.5 meters thick, the ceilings 3.5 meters. The Flak tower could offer safety to 18,000 people; other sources even cite 50- to 60,000 as its capacity. It had five upper stories, two main and four auxiliary entrances. In the fourth upper story were quarters for the Luftwaffe women helpers as well as the Warning Command (WaKo) and the Aircraft Spotting Command (FluKo). The harbor hospital and the Reichspost had their facilities below. The kitchen facilities were located between Towers 1 and 4. In the fifth upper story were quarters for the Luftwaffe helpers and the crews of the "Anton", "Berta", Cäsar" and "Dora" Flak guns (1/414), between Towers 1 and 2.*

The Flak tower's armament consisted of four 128 mm Flak guns in twin mounts, as well as fifteen 37 mm Flak on the lower platform. They belonged to a unit of the 3rd Flak Division. In the Gomorrha attacks, the 128 mm Flak guns fired a total of 9192 rounds, with more than 3000 in 1944. Between October 13, 1942 and March 31, 1945 the 1./414 (T) is said to have shot down fifty planes.

Attempts by the Director of the City Archives to house valuable city archives in the gun tower failed, although space was promised him on July 25, 1943. This space could not be used for the city archives because it was occupied by homeless people. The space for art treasures, though, was already included in the plans: Towers 2 and 3 in the second upper story were chosen for that purpose.

On May 5, 1945, the British took over the administration of the Heiligengeistfeld Flak tower. The "Abwicklungsamt Wehrmacht" approved the freeing of the Flak tower for civilian use on March 13, 1946. On April 1, 1946, the Oberfinanzpräsident took over the administration of the bunker. As of August 20, 1946, the Flak tower could be fitted with windows for dwellings. On December 28, 1948, the occupying powers were given detailed plans for the decommissioning of the Flak tower and the removal of the dwellings; no objections were made.

In 1956, "Hochhaus II" became a "creative bunker" when the world-renowned fashion photographer F. C. Gundlach located his studio and workrooms there.

In 1975, fifteen firms were registered in the G-tower, particularly those in photography and advertising. In 1986, 25 firms occupied 13,000 square meters of the Flak tower.

*See variations in floor utilization, previous page.

### Bremen-Neustadt

On October 28, 1942, the Reich Governor in Oldenburg and Bremen, Senator Dr. Fischer, met the director of the air-protection construction department, Baurat Assmann, the commander of the 8th Flak Division, Generalleutnant Wagner, and Building Engineer Bockmann of the Luftwaffe Building Department in the "House of the Reich" in Bremen for an inspection trip. After the heavy air raids on Bremen, a Flak tower was to be built in the green belt of the free Hanseatic city [page 27] between the Neustadt-Contrescarpe, Laibnizstrasse and Richthofenstrasse. The construction was regarded as not big enough to make special city planning necessary.

The Reichs Ministry of Speer, the GB Air Protection Building Office and the OT had agreed. To be sure, building the bunker in Bremen was not to be taken on by these offices; the offices carrying out the job were to obtain workers and building materials themselves. It was decided to make deep borings in order to solidify the varying terrain in that part of the city. An inspection trip to Hamburg, where two pairs of Flak towers already existed, was to be made early in November 1942. But only the planning was done in Bremen, and Flak towers were never built.

*Interior construction of the Heiligengeistfeld gun tower.*

*20 mm Flak quads on the Heiligengeistfeld L-tower in Hamburg.*

The two-meter reinforced concrete wall of the G-tower can be seen clearly here. At right are the outside stairs from the lower to the upper platform.

Here the Heiligengeist-feld tower is still partly painted in a dark color. Towers I (left) and 4 (right) can be seen. This side faced the command tower.

*The Heiligengeistfeld G-tower, protected by barrage balloons. The 128 mm Flak 40 guns in twin mounts are already in position. Some wooden scaffolds and barracks can be seen. The light areas indicate the future windows (see below) and frames for the steel blinds (small photo).*

From the upper platform of the Heiligengeistfeld G-tower, the Hamburg television tower can be seen in the background. In the foreground is one of four concrete structures for equipment, ammunition and cleaning supplies. Below: a base for the twin mount of the 128 mm heavy Flak guns.

*Above: the Diesel engine for the freight elevator.*
*Upper right: the cellar of the G-tower, lined with brick.*
*Right: the ammunition chambers.*
*Lower right: the typical spiral staircase of the four corner towers of the first four Flak towers, on which thousands of civilians sat during air raids.*
*Below: probably one of the Luftwaffe command rooms in the G-tower.*
*(All photos taken 9/26/1994)*

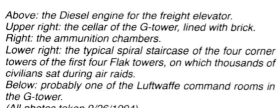

*A model of the Heiligengeistfeld L-tower, and (lower left) the tower itself when almost finished.*

*The Telekom building which occupies the site of the former L-tower today.*

Upper left: Shortly after a 1973 explosion, the upper platform has already been reduced to large chunks by explosives. After a few floors in between had been demolished, the rubble was dumped down the shaft, some 12 meters deep, of the "Würzburg Giant" inside the L-tower. This job was done by a bulldozer that had been lifted to the lower platform by a crane. An opening 6 meters wide and 3.5 meters high had been blown in the outer wall, through which a bulldozer could get inside the L-tower and remove the rubble at night. The Oxygen Spreng- und Baugesellschaft, which had been given the job, estimated 225 work days for breaking down the ceilings and inner walls, 400 days for breaking down the entire structure to the level of the top of the foundation, and 55 days for breaking down the bunker foundation. But twenty men needed only 330 work days to remove the concrete giant. In all, 280 tons of structural iron were salvaged.

Right: Holes for explosive charges are bored in the concrete with oxygen torches. The explosions themselves were carried out so that a sewer running 13 meters under the foundation was not damaged. The roof of the St. Pauli Clubhouse nearby was reinforced with timbers. In all, 300 charges were planned, one for almost every work day.

Lower left: With a crane, a Liebherr 921 LC hydraulic excavator was lifted onto the upper platform to remove the roof. The mass of rubble amounted to 30,400 cubic meters in all. The G-tower can be seen at the right in the picture.

Lower right: The shaft for the "Würzburg Giant" radar device, which was used for interior demolition. The amount of rubble removed daily was 100 cubic meters.

*The G-tower on Neuhoferstrasse in Hamburg-Wilhelmsburg. Below the lower platform, the concrete walls show signs of wear. Photographed in 1996.*

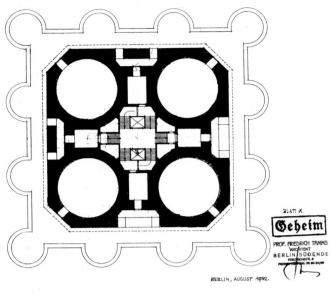

PLAN A.
**Geheim**
PROF. FRIEDRICH TAMMS
ARCHITEKT
BERLIN SÜDENDE
FRIEDRICHSTR. 8
FERNSPRECHER: 75 90 94/95

BERLIN, AUGUST 1942.

In a version planned by Dr. Tamms (left), there were two additional "swallows' nests" foreseen on each side between those at the corners. These were not built, presumably for reasons of economy. The model (above) shows the new generation of Flak towers (G) with half-covered Flak positions (Wilhelmsburg-Arenberg Park model).

The new Flak-tower generation (the Wilhelmsburg-Arenbergpark G-tower) with the gun positions half-covered by concrete ceilings on the round turrets. Unlike the first four Flak towers, the steps to the upper platform are not exposed outside, but are covered by concrete. The crane on rails on the upper platform is a new feature.

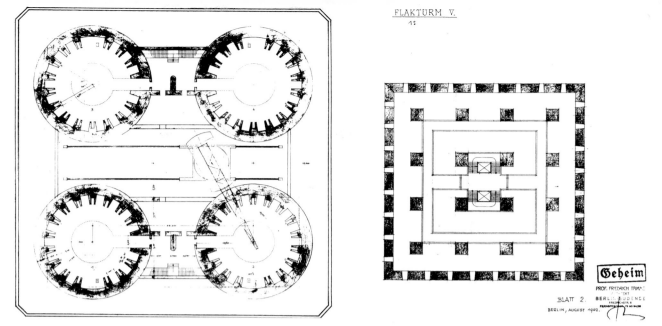

© H. W. Tamms (2)

© O. Wleklinski

Upper left: layout of the upper platform with crane. The opening in the concrete covering for the resting position 0 of the Flak gun is 2.3 meters wide. The midpoints of Towers 1 and 2 are exactly 30 meters away from each other. Below: The maneuvering space of the Flak-gun barrel (10 to 87 degrees) measures 4 meters. The small chambers under the concrete top are for shell casings, the large ones for Flak ammunition. The freight and ammunition elevators, though, were not installed, so that the 128 mm shells had to be carried laboriously from the ammunition storerooms to the guns by Luftwaffe helpers. Upper right: Floor plan of a floor in the gun tower, by Prof. Tamms in August 1942. Not all of the many window openings were built. The G-tower had a surface area of 57 x 57 meters and was 41.6 meters high. The roof was 3.5 meters thick. In mid-1943 the 128 mm twin Flak guns were installed. Up to 30,000 people are said to have found shelter from air raids here.

On October 17, 1947, the interior of the Wilhelmsburg G-tower was demolished by explosions. Anyone living within 500 meters was evacuated, and 600 police were sent to close off the area.

The "Hamburger Freie Presse" wrote on October 18, 1947: "Exactly at 11:00 AM, the first sign of the explosion, a fiery, smoky glow shot out of the east-side window of the bunker under great pressure. It was followed immediately by the detonation, awesome, dark and dull. . . . With one stroke, the gigantic concrete block of 65,000 cubic meters came alive. . . ." Lower right: Dust flies out of the east window and rises above the terrace.

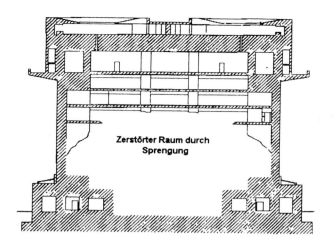

Zerstörter Raum durch
Sprengung

© O. Wlekinski

© O. Wlekinski (3)

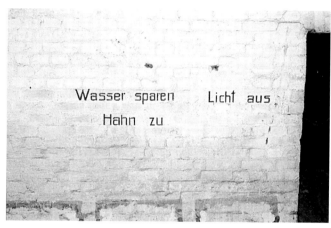

Wasser sparen    Licht aus
Hahn zu

Weitergehen

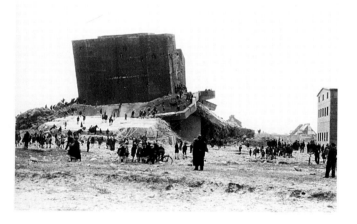

When the smoke of the explosion had cleared and the Wilhelmsburg G-tower became visible, apparently almost unscathed, spectators are said to have cried, "Made in Germany! Made in Germany!" But the British wanted to destroy the interior, and succeeded in doing so.

Right: The explosion tore the cement roof off.

Left center: A destroyed flight of stairs with steps fallen down.

Right center and lower left: Writing on the walls.
After the explosion, the stasis had changed; it was hardly possible for the G-tower to be included in a new building project.

Lower right: Explosion of the L-tower on October 10, 1947. An eyewitness report: "As the clock struck 11:00 AM, a mighty detonation shook the Wilhelmsburg part of the city. A dark cloud of smoke enveloped the bunker for minutes. The colossus, formerly 44 meters high and 38 meters long, had changed its shape strikingly. The outside walls, 3.5 meters thick, did not withstand the explosion of 8500 kilograms. Yet they limited the effect of the explosion so much that there was no damage to even the nearest apartment houses. The bunker was turned to a heap of rubble, which probably gave the disposal office a lot of trouble and added a lot to the volume of rubble in Hamburg."

## Vienna

Hitler himself, in September 1942 (according to other sources, on November 9, 1942), had ordered the construction of two pairs of Flak towers in Vienna, since in his opinion one of the most important city centers, that of Vienna, should be protected. Even after 4000 years, they should remind future generations of the struggle of the Third Reich. In the Luftwaffe's opinion, they should be built on the Schmelz, in the Prater and in Florisdorf (three sites), but Hitler himself decided on the locations. Flak Tower VIII (identical to the Wilhelmsburg Flak tower in Hamburg) was to be built in the Arenberg Park, Flak Tower V in the Stiftskaserne. Flak Tower VII, if the Führer wished, would be built near the Rossau Barracks, but was built in the Augarten. Thus, three G-towers with their L-towers were built in all.

The plans for the Vienna Flak towers were likewise drawn by Professor Dipl.Ing. Friedrich Tamms, born in Schwerin in 1904; he was a city planner who had attracted attention with his super-highway and bridge designs. The building of the Flak towers was supervised by the Ministry of Armament in Berlin, Military Construction Department. The first plans for the Vienna Flak towers were destroyed in an air raid on Berlin. Dipl.Ing. Ruschitzka had to prepare new plans in Vienna within two days.

The Flak towers were positioned in a triangle, so that the shot values of the heavy Flak, which Prof. Tamms estimated at 20 to 22 kilometers, overlapped. The locations themselves were determined by the City of Vienna and the LGK. The sites were selected so that, as Tamms said, "the inner city can be defended against air attacks—including low-flying planes." "Test facilities" were built in Unterlüss for series of tests.

All the L-towers, like those in Germany, were rectangular, though with smaller dimensions (31 x 18 meters, or 50 x 23 according to other data), but the Stiftskaserne and Augarten gun towers, with sixteen sides, were practically round.

On every tower, 300 to 500 foreign workers were employed, particularly Yugoslavs and Greeks, but also Italian military internees and a few Austrian skilled workers. There were also construction units of the RAD and the Wehrmacht, as well as Jewish forced laborers. The building materials were brought to the building sites on newly-laid rail lines, sometimes even on streetcars, from the Danube and the Aspang depot.

The Viennese Flak towers were built on concrete slabs at least two meters thick. A very hard type of concrete, reinforced with spirals, was used. The outer walls were two meters thick, the roofs up to 3.5 meters. On the towers themselves, cranes were mounted, sometimes on rails which had been mounted on the roof to give them flexibility to serve all four 128 mm gun mounts. The building time was half a year, and the last tower to be ready for action, in the early summer of 1944, was the Stiftskaserne gun tower.

No tower was completely finished, though all were ready for action by the summer of 1944.

The gun mounts were similar to those of the Wilhelmsburg Flak tower. The crews of the 128 mm Flak guns were somewhat safe from splinters and light bombs hitting the roof because of the fact that the guns in the towers were protected by steel cupolas.

In the upper third of the gun towers, lower platforms for light Flak weapons were built, though they never actually seem to have been installed. Every bunker had a water supply and its own powerplant. They were used as storehouses for valuable cultural objects, housed military offices, and 15,000 civilians found shelter there at times. In all the gun towers there were hospitals, some with more than 800 beds. Armament industries were likewise housed in the Flak towers, where they produced aircraft engines, electrical parts and ammunition.

The "Würzburg Giant" and a small "Würzburg" device or a "Mannheim" type radar device were installed on all three L-towers. There was also a Command Device 40 with a six-meter range finder.

The Flak towers in Vienna were also included in Architect Tamms' considerations for city planning. The Stiftskaserne Flak tower thus stood exactly on the axis of the Vienna Castle and the Augarten towers stood in Vienna's oldest Baroque garden.

Since it was known that a removal of concrete masses would be impossible after the "final victory", the Flak towers were supposed to be finished in the style of the medieval Hohenstaufen castles in Germany and Italy, with raw tiles and French marble, lying ready in quarries near Lyon, Paris and Orleans. Its transport never took place, on account of the Allied landing in Normandy.

. The Flak bunkers in Vienna are believed to have proved themselves. In the 7th District of Vienna, where the Stiftskaserne tower stood, there was the least bomb damage in Vienna, with "only" 107 air-raid fatalities listed. Still in all, Architect Tamms estimated after the war that the "shooting cathedrals" had not fulfilled the expected military hopes that one originally had for them. And Jan Tabor said: "Without wanting to deny the military purposefulness of these buildings completely, they were conceived from the beginning and above all as 'mood architecture'." The designer compared them with the Egyptian pyramids: "They are monuments of and for all times. As a result, they are without utilitarian value in the usual sense. They are as useless as plastic art. But they were carriers of an idea, an elementary feeling for power, stability and will to live."

As in Berlin, the Vienna Flak towers took part in the final combat around the Austrian capital and fired on Russian troop concentrations near the attack routes in the south, southeast and west sides of the city. There the units of the 3rd and 9th Guard Armies gathered, as well as the 6th Armored Guard Army. The 2nd Battery on the Stiftskaserne gun tower fired barrage fire as far as Laxenburg, Hennersdorf, Perchtoldsdorf, Rodaun and Mauer. The air pressure broke windows in all the surrounding area, and the window frames were loosened in the barracks. The 1st Battery on the Arenberg Flak tower fired barrage fire at ground targets in southern Vienna on April 4, 1945. The Luftwaffe helpers at these batteries, as well as the woman Flak helpers, had already been discharged. Firing continued steadily for four days and nights.

As opposed to Berlin, where all the Flak towers have been destroyed except what remains of the Humboldthain gun tower, all the towers in Vienna have been retained. As early as 1946, Prof.Dr. Karl Krupsky thought of beautifying the concrete structures. In 1951 Prof. Erwin Bock considered resurfacing the towers, as was originally intended, and in 1953 the idea [p. 39] of turning the Flak towers into large parking garages came up. To this day, none of these projects has been carried out. In 1990 the flak towers, owned by the Austrian Republic, were given to the City of Vienna.

## Arenberg Park

The G- and L- tower in the Arenberg Park were built in the summer of 1943 and manned by the 1st Battery of Tower Flak Unit 184. The Flak tower covered an area of 57 x 57 meters and was identical to the Wilhelmsburg gun tower in Hamburg. The gun tower was armed with four 105 mm Flak guns, and as of January 1944 with four 128 mm Flak, then with four of the same caliber in twin mounts.

After the last shells were fired in the final combat of 1945, the guns and technical equipment were blown up on the 8th floor. The crews of the flak towers left the bunker on April 8, 1945. There had been no shortage of ammunition; even after the surrender, large supplies of Flak shells remained in the bunkers.

Today the gun tower is used as a storehouse (art depot) and the L-tower stands empty.

Above: the Arenberg Park gun tower, identical to the Wilhelmsburg G-tower in Hamburg.

Left: a model of the Arenberg Park L-tower.

Right: the Arenberg Park L-tower, identical to the Wilhelmsburg L-tower, as seen in May 1996.

© M. Mildschuh

**Hinweisschriften im G-Turm Arenbergpark.**

The chimney of the heating plant for the Arenberg Park gun tower.

Left: the Arenberg Park L-tower; the door to the shaft for lowering the "Würzburg Giant".

Above: a room near the main entrance of the Arenberg Park gun tower.
Left: the ammunition delivery system in a position on the gun tower.

## Stiftskaserne

In the grounds of the Stiftskaserne, the gun tower was built from May to September 1943, and the 2nd Battery of Tower Flak unit 184 was stationed on it. The L-tower was some 500 meters away in Esterhazy Park. The Flak tower here, with an overall height of 45 meters, was the lowest in Vienna. Having sixteen sides, it was almost round, and measured 43 meters in diameter. The gun tower was armed with four 128 mm Flak 44 guns in twin mounts. The guns were protected from enemy fire by steel cupolas.

After 1945 the gun tower was used by the American occupation troops and later reactivated as an atom-bomb bunker, presumably one of the government's two bunkers. The gun tower is used by the Austrian Army today.

The L-tower in the Esterhazy Park had a cellar, a ground floor and twelve upper stories. The tower is said to have taken a bomb hit on the uppermost platform. Whether light Flak guns were stationed on the lower platform cannot be said for sure. Here, too, there are opposing statements. Since 1958 the L-tower has been used in part by the "House of the Sea" as a sea museum, where a shark swims in an aquarium. In 1961 a man jumped down a 12-meter-deep air shaft to his death. In order to remove the body, the firemen had to break through a wall. Again and again, scurrilous plans turned up, such as building a cableway on the L-tower. Packaging artist Christo planned to wrap the L-tower in 1995, but this was not approved.

*A model of the Easterhazy Park L-tower, showing the north side.*

*The south side of the Esterhazy Park L-tower with the opening for the crane, the focal point and concrete counterweight of which can be seen. On the left side was the "Würzburg Giant"; its shaft is covered with sheet metal today. The projecting "swallows' nests", unlike those of the Augarten L-tower, had no supports.*

The lower and upper platforms of the Stiftskaserne gun tower. The radar devices are unknown to the author.

Left page: Aerial view of the gun tower. The main entrance was on the left side.

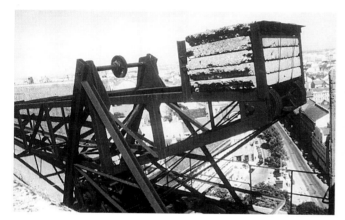

Upper left: the crane with its counterweight in resting position on the upper platform of the Esterhazy Park L-tower.
Above: the covered shaft of the "Würzburg Giant".
Left center: the position of the Command Device 40 (steel frame built after the war).
Lower left: view over Vienna to the Vienna Woods from the lower platform of the Esterhazy Park L-tower.
Below: view to the northwest from the upper platform of the Esterhazy Park L-tower, position hf the Command Device 40, and at left the access to the stairs to the lower floors. There the L-tower is used by the Sea museum; sharks, snakes and crocodiles can be seen in aquariums and terrariums.

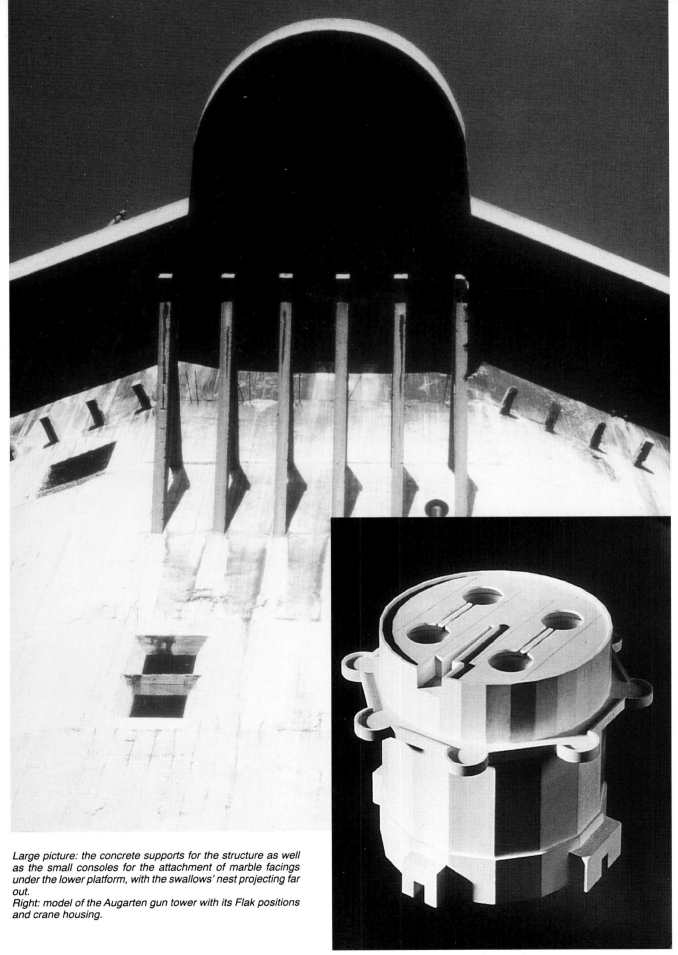

Large picture: the concrete supports for the structure as well as the small consoles for the attachment of marble facings under the lower platform, with the swallows' nest projecting far out.
Right: model of the Augarten gun tower with its Flak positions and crane housing.

On the Augarten gun tower: at left the support for the resting position of the 128 mm twin Flak guns. Right: the opening in the upper platform for the crane's resting position.

## Augarten

In the Augarten, the G- and L-towers were manned by the 3rd Battery of Tower Flak Unit 184. At 50.5 (by other data 54) meters, it was the tallest of the Viennese Flak towers. It was almost round, with sixteen sides, and measured 43 meters in diameter. The outer walls were 2.5 meters thick. Some ten meters below the top, a platform, five meters wide with extending corners (swallows' nests), runs around the tower. The G-tower was armed with four 128 mm Flak 44 in twin mounts.

In the G-tower, radio tubes were produced, and the mayor and his staff had offices and workrooms in the gun tower. In the park between the G- and L-towers, barracks for the Flak helpers and "lightning girls" were built.

In the last combat in April 1945, the L-tower was hit by at least three Soviet artillery shells, all striking the upper third of the tower and one breaking through the outer wall.

The "Österreichische Zeitung" reported on November 22, 1946, that children had played "war" in the Flak tower the day before, using a fuse to explode two wagonloads of Flak ammunition. The result was a crack in the north wall. Nobody was killed or injured, and the children remain unknown to this day. According to another report, several children from the neighboring area went missing that day and never appeared again.

The Russians tried to blow up the gun tower, leaving traces clearly visible to this day.

The Augarten towers were walled up after the war.

Entrance to the Augarten gun tower "only for military personnel in uniform".

Damage done by the Soviets is easy to see in the Augarten gun tower. Gigantic concrete blocks were torn out of the insides of the walls. Right: the size can be seen clearly. The gun tower is inhabited by pigeons, which fly inside through openings in the outer walls.

Position of the 128 mm twin Flak guns, with base and breech rest.

The Augarten gun tower as seen in 1994. The appearance of the tower, then still painted a dark camouflage color, has changed much since then, as wind and weather have removed almost all the paint, leaving a lighter surface. The tower was first planned with nine floors, which were then increased to twelve.

The gun tower's height is 54 meters! Since a frame of that height would have collapsed under its own weight at that time, and the expense would have been too great if the swallows' nests had been damaged, consoles were built into the outside walls under the lower platform to allow further work in case of bomb damage. The consoles were also built under the lower platform of the Augarten L-tower, since it was about the same height as the gun tower.

Right: 128 mm twin Flak guns in a gun position on the Augarten gun tower. The concrete roof protects the gunners from enemy fire.

The Augarten L-tower, seen from the lower platform of the G-tower. Although the view was limited in such weather, there were no problems with optical contact. Right: When the Red Army reached Vienna and the Augarten towers in April 1945, heavy artillery fire was begun. The picture shows the hole in the wall above the lower platform, behind which was the reevaluating room with the "Malsi Devices". Penetration was possible because the outer walls of the L-tower at this height were less than one meter thick.

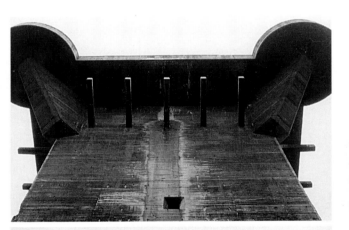

Upper left: the north side of the L-tower, also still painted black when photographed in 1994. Note the strong supports under the swallows' nests.
Right: two years later, by which time the L-tower had become markedly lighter.
Left: On the upper platform of the L-tower, apparently part of a mount for a radar device.